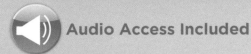

Easy INSTRUMENTAL PLAY-ALONG

Audio Access Included

Visit **www.halleonard.com/mylibrary**

Enter Code

4798-7601-2862-8819

CLASSICAL THEMES
FOR TENOR SAX

T0070585

CONTENTS

Audio Arrangements by Peter Deneff
Tracking, mixing, and mastering by BeatHouse Music

ISBN 978-1-4803-6050-1

7777 W. BLUEMOUND RD. P.O. BOX 13819 MILWAUKEE, WI 53213

In Australia Contact:
Hal Leonard Australia Pty. Ltd.
4 Lentara Court
Cheltenham, Victoria, 3192 Australia
Email: ausadmin@halleonard.com.au

For all works contained herein:
Unauthorized copying, arranging, adapting, recording, Internet posting, public performance,
or other distribution of the printed or recorded music in this publication is an infringement of copyright.
Infringers are liable under the law.

Visit Hal Leonard Online at
www.halleonard.com

FINLANDIA

Copyright © 2013 by HAL LEONARD CORPORATION
International Copyright Secured   All Rights Reserved

By JEAN SIBELIUS

MORNING

from PEER GYNT

Copyright © 2013 by HAL LEONARD CORPORATION
International Copyright Secured   All Rights Reserved

By EDVARD GRIEG

SYMPHONY NO. 1
Fourth Movement Excerpt

Copyright © 2013 by HAL LEONARD CORPORATION
International Copyright Secured   All Rights Reserved

By JOHANNES BRAHMS

CARNIVAL OF VENICE

Copyright © 2013 by HAL LEONARD CORPORATION
International Copyright Secured   All Rights Reserved

By JULIUS BENEDICT

SPRING
from THE FOUR SEASONS

Copyright © 2013 by HAL LEONARD CORPORATION
International Copyright Secured   All Rights Reserved

By ANTONIO VIVALDI

CAN CAN
from ORPHEUS IN THE UNDERWORLD

Copyright © 2013 by HAL LEONARD CORPORATION
International Copyright Secured   All Rights Reserved

By JACQUES OFFENBACH

MUSETTE
from THE ANNA MAGDALENA NOTEBOOK

Copyright © 2013 by HAL LEONARD CORPORATION
International Copyright Secured   All Rights Reserved

By JOHANN SEBASTIAN BACH

TRUMPET VOLUNTARY
(Prince of Denmark's March)

Copyright © 2013 by HAL LEONARD CORPORATION
International Copyright Secured   All Rights Reserved

By JEREMIAH CLARKE

8

LARGO
from SYMPHONY NO. 9 ("New World")

Copyright © 2013 by HAL LEONARD CORPORATION
International Copyright Secured   All Rights Reserved

By ANTONIN DVOŘÁK

ODE TO JOY
from SYMPHONY NO. 9

Copyright © 2013 by HAL LEONARD CORPORATION
International Copyright Secured   All Rights Reserved

By LUDWIG VAN BEETHOVEN